There's Something in the Garden

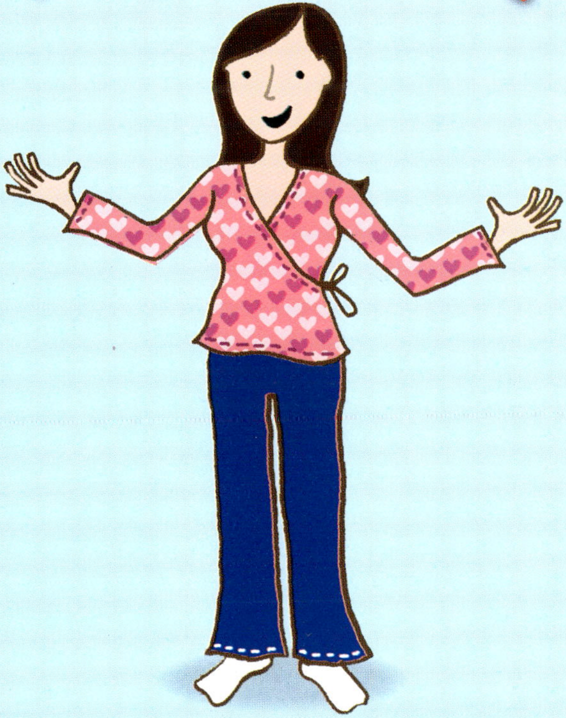

Written by Paul Shipton
Illustrated by Jessie Eckle

Will sat up.
“There’s something in the garden,” he said. “It’s a monster. I can see a monster!”

"Me too!" Cath said. "It's big with long arms."

"That's just a tree," Mum said.

Will sat up again.
“I can hear a monster,” he said.

“So can I! It’s growling,” Cath said.
“That’s just the dog,” Mum said.

“I can smell a monster!” Will said.
“So can I!” Cath said.

"You can smell Dad's coffee. It is NOT a monster. Now go to sleep!" said Mum.

But there was a big monster in the garden.
And a little monster, too.

The little monster said,
"There's something in the garden.
It's a kid. I can hear a kid!"

“That’s just a cat,” said the big monster.

But the little monster said,
"I can see a kid. Look!"

“That’s just a bush,” said the big monster.

But the little monster said,
"I can smell a kid!"

"No, you can smell the flowers,"
the big monster said.
But then ...

Sniff! Sniff!
“Wait! I can smell kids, too!”
he said.

"And they STINK! Let's go!"